Change Your Mind and You Change Your Life

by

Dr. Vanessa Lynn Estes

Dedication

I like to dedicate this book to the memory of my mother, Mary Evelyn Buchanan-Jones, who told me to never give up; my grandparents, Jack and Anna Turner, who knew the Lord's hands were always on me for greater works and my big brother, Gregory Anthony Estes, who always protected me.

Mary Buchanan-Jones   **Gregory Estes**

Jack Turner   **Anna Turner**

Special Thanks

I want to honor God, who is the head of my life and the one I seek daily for wisdom, strength, and knowledge. If it had not been for Him, His *Grace,* and *Mercy*, I would not be able to share my testimony of *"Life"* with the world. I would also like to thank my mother, the late Mary Evelyn Buchanan-Jones, for her guidance; and Mother Ollie Nance Thomas, Third Baptist Church in Detroit Michigan, for inspiring me to write; and my best friend and spiritual advisor, Minister Judith Randolph, for encouraging me when I came to the crossroads in my life. Special thanks to my children, Allen, Zeberida, and Evelyn, for having patience with me in the ministry. Most of all, I would like to thank Chief Apostle Paulette Alston (Glorified God Church of Deliverance – 8601), Detroit, Michigan, for showing and teaching me about the love of God, but mainly the power God has given us to do all things when we are anointed by Christ. And to my best friend, Pastor Glinda Harris, on the teachings of how to live on earth while we wait to live again with God.

Contents

Preface

2 Timothy 1:7

> For God hath not given us the spirit of fear; but of power, and of love, and of a sound mind.

The mind, heart, and soul are delicate tools we need to survive daily. However, let these tools get into the wrong hands, the hands of the enemy, and you can have a problem too big to handle. This is why changing the way you think can change your life. Now I understand the Scripture in Deuteronomy 6:5, "And thou shalt love the LORD thy God with all thine heart, and with all thy soul, and with all thy might."[1] This is a powerful verse. When we love God with our entire being, we become one with Him, and therefore we can have inner peace, the kind of peace that you cannot explain to any man. It is a peace that keeps you calm and puts you at rest in the arms of Jesus. This peace is *priceless.*

I suffered from anxiety stress disorder for many years. When people looked at me, they had no clue of the demon I fought daily, warring inside my head. A demon I kept to myself and hid from the world, including my family. No one knew the hell that I suffered daily. I felt that keeping quiet was best because no one would understand. Or I felt they would think I was insane and judge me; either way, it was my demon to fight. After years of fighting this battle

---

[1] All Scripture is of the King James Version unless otherwise stated.

1

of fear, I told my mom I had written this blog. She was stunned that I had gone through this ordeal without her knowledge, wondering why I did not mention it to her.

Many people are going through the same things I suffered; panic attacks, depression, night sweats, rapid heart beating, insomnia, headaches, backaches, brain fog, tingling in hands/arms, etc. The list could go on and on. Sometimes you feel like you are on a roller coaster ride and want to get off. Allow me to say one important thing: You are not crazy. No, it is not fun; however, you are not alone. Many people go through depression, and may ask themselves, what is going on with my mind? Too afraid to say something because of being committed due to insanity. [According to the *World Health Organization,* more than 264 million people worldwide suffer from depression.] No one wants to be labeled as having a mental disorder, minimized, or taunted. So, you keep quiet and pray that God will deliver you from the hell of depression.

Over the years, I have learned one thing about the body: your mind controls everything. "For as he thinketh in his heart, so is he (Prov. 23:7)." We are in control of our thoughts and become what we think. Do not allow your heart, mind, and soul to be captivated by the visions and distracted by the enemy, which can separate us from God. You have heard the saying, believe half of what you see and none of what you hear! I am saying that people listen to what they want: Yes, it is up to you to have faith in what you believe, regardless of the circumstances around you; consider that.

Do not store up treasures in the world with deceitful thinking. It can lead to living in sin against God. "For where your treasure is, there will your heart be also (Matt. 6:21)." Our hearts cannot serve two masters: living a worldly lifestyle and living for God. And because I tried to do this, my sins against God sowed fear. However, my fear controlled the very thing God wanted us to love Him with, *our entire mind.*

We cannot live outside the will of God and not expect the devil to walk into His place. The enemy waits every second of your life, trying to destroy what God has created in His image. "Be sober, be vigilant; because your adversary the devil, as a roaring lion, walketh about, seeking whom he may devour (1 Pet. 5:8)." And the very moment we feel comfortable in being away from God, the enemy comes swiftly to steal your joy, peace, and the most fragile and valuable part of your body that doctors have said we cannot function without, *your mind.*

Those of you suffering from these symptoms, please join me in renewing your mind. We will fight this demon together, one step at a time, one day at a time. If you do not want to, you do not have to fight for your life. However, I refused to let negative thoughts enter my mind and take control of my body. I did not want to live in agony and discomfort for the rest of my life. I pray and hope that together I can help renew the minds of those seeking a life of abundance so that we can live a fulfilling life pleasing to the Lord. "I can do all things through Christ which strengtheneth me (Phil 4:13)."

There are instructions that I follow to have a renewed mind. They have helped me in the mind renewal process. It may seem challenging initially to take all these steps; however, I had to start somewhere. It was hard for me at first, yet I did not want the devil to have victory over my mind. When you defeat the enemy, your first weapon that will hurt him is the word *TRY*. My grandmother always said this to me, Nothing beats a failure but a *TRY*. You have already failed if you do not *TRY*.

Introduction

This book is a blog that I wrote when I was going through the storms of life. Below are instructions I used daily to have my mind refreshed and rejuvenated. Only apply yourself to do these exercises if you feel it is manageable. Moreover, always seek medical advice from your physician before starting any exercise regimen. You will understand the process of renewing your mind after going through the fire and coming back. And I promise you we will do this together. This is not just for the moment; this is exercise for a lifetime of joy!

Steps to a Renewed Mind

1. Every morning, get out of bed. Yes, make yourself get out of bed. Because you have everything to live for and a purpose for living; your children, your spouse, and mainly you, YOU NEED YOU! So, stop having a pity party and join me in this thing we call Life. "For I know the thoughts that I think toward you, saith the Lord, thoughts of peace, and not of evil, to give you an expected end (Jer. 29:11)." God is expecting you to start the plans that He has set up for you. He knows the outcome will be good and not evil because He will see it through. You must have that NOW faith and get started.

2. Meditate and pray for at least 15 minutes or more each morning. If you work and do not have the time, you can pray on the way to work by listening to a prayer CD in your car. Or if you take public transportation, you can close your eyes and

meditate or listen to soothing music on an iPod. Once your mind is in a positive mode, concentrate only on pleasant thoughts throughout the day.

3. **TRY** to think about something funny, something that amused you earlier in the week, or words someone spoke that encouraged you. Going to the spa and getting a massage works wonders, TRY it. Moreover, to relax at night, TRY listening to soothing music while meditating or taking a hot bubble bath. Turn off any distractions, i.e., phones, TVs, video games, computers, and so on. *Relaxation* is refreshing your body, mind, and soul, so avoid any distractions. After all, the end of the day should be yours to enjoy.

4. Eating unhealthily can be a factor that may cause depression. Not having the proper nutrients or lacking vitamins can be a health risk. The mind needs the energy to stay focused. I began drinking flavored soymilk when I was going through hot flashes. Vitamins are a must to ensure you get proper nutrients. [*Please seek medical advice before taking any vitamins or changing your diet, especially if you are on any medications or have any medical conditions.*][2]

5. Exercise if you can. Walking is excellent exercise, and it can be fun. Start with 5-10 minutes daily, then work your way up according to how you feel (with the advice of a medical

---

[2] Always seek the advice of your physician if you want to start a vitamin regimen, diet, or exercise program. I am not a medical doctor; I only give out spiritual advice based on the Bible and through the direction of the Holy Spirit.

professional), especially if you are stressed. Walking helps clear the mind, and it is not strenuous. Starting slowly is particularly good because you want to avoid overexerting yourself. [*Before you begin any exercise regimen, seek medical advice.*]

6. Make a list of everything you want to do when you have time. NO! You are going to be available for your life. Regardless of how difficult you think it might be to create a list! Maybe you wanted to become an actor/actress, singer, musician, etc. Mark off what you have accomplished and then decide on things you want to complete. The things in your life you always wanted to do, yet you procrastinated. Pray and ask God to direct your path, and He will answer you in due season. When is your due season? When God feels that you are ready. Keep pursuing the vision that God has for you. It is closer than you realize. It is your faith that will make you whole. If you do not believe in yourself, how do you expect others to?

7. "The Lord answered me, and said, Write the vision, and make it plain upon tables, that he may run that readeth it (Hab. 2:2)." Run with the gifts God has given you. Remember, I am right here with you in spirit. We are doing this together.

8. Make a daily to-do list or create a monthly calendar that includes your household obligations, lunch/dinner menu preparations, doctor appointments, etc. I made one, and it is the best thing I have ever done. This will help keep you organized and less stressed. God is all about order. "Let all

things be done decently and in order (1 Cor. 14:40)." Do not forget to treat yourself for all your daily efforts. It does not have to be anything costly. You can treat yourself to a small bowl of ice cream, rest, or close your eyes and think of how good God has been to you. Take care of #1, *YOU*, first. You are important to you. Enjoy *your* life.

9. You may not be a people person or outspoken; however, try speaking to people when you are out by saying hello or have a lovely day. Also, calling a special friend will not only put a smile on their face but will uplift your spirit. As we encourage ourselves, let us learn to encourage someone else. Why? Someone may be going through challenging times as well, and a friendly smile or a word of encouragement could be the very thing that might keep them motivated.

10. Stay positive, with no negativity. Just stay focused on enjoying life. The life that God has given you. If family members or friends with problems need to talk, tell them you will speak to them later, or let it go to voicemail. Schedule a day or time, depending on the seriousness of the situation, to discuss problems/issues with family and friends and handle things in your own time. Because life does exist, and we cannot ignore negativity forever. We just cannot stay in it long because it will drag us down.

11. Lastly, always remember to pray and read the Bible daily. Because when you *Change Your Mind, You Change Your Life!*

These instructions should start you on the way to having a refreshed state of being. Later, you may create your own rules for relaxation. You cannot manage everything alone, so let God take care of the rest. Always make sure that you pray before making any decisions. Then seek and wait for an answer from God. After your day of overcoming your difficulties in life, go back to focusing on the positive. Take a nice soothing bath to relax your muscles, turn on soothing music, read a book, do whatever it takes to calm your nerves, and relax your mind. I pray these steps help you find the peace of mind you deserve. As we move forward, the rest of the book is to help you understand who I am and how I achieved to regain peace in my life through my many blogs. May God bless you, and remember, *Change Your Mind & You Change Your Life!*

Intro to Blogs - New Beginnings

Happy Father's Day

Sunday: June 20, 2010

Being raised by a single mother is extremely hard, which most people know is true. However, being raised without a father puts a more complex strain on a child. I can relate to President Obama saying: I was raised without my father. Yes, my father and I talked when I became an adult and had my own family. However, he was not there for me when I was young. He and my mother divorced when I was five.

I wanted my father to live in the house with me so badly. Not realizing that what I wanted were not the plans that God intended for my life, and His plans were most important. I was angry with my dad for many years. Moreover, I needed to move forward with my life, so I forgave my father because God forgave me for all my sins. When you let go and accept change, it will relieve you and set you free. "But if ye forgive not men their trespasses, neither will your Father forgive your trespasses (Matt. 6:15)." Some people go through depression and a heavy heart because they carry the extra baggage of unforgiveness. People hurt is painful, yet God's love is powerful. If you want the blessings of the Lord and His forgiveness, you must *LET GO!* Below is an email that I received on Father's Day from President Obama on my White House Blog that I would like to share with everyone:

Good afternoon,

As the father of two young daughters, I know that being a father is one of the most important jobs any man can have.

My father left my family when I was two years old. I was raised by a heroic mother and wonderful grandparents who provided the support, discipline, and love that helped me get to where I am today, but I still felt the weight of that absence throughout my childhood. It is something that leaves a hole no government can fill. Studies show that children who grow up without their fathers around them are more likely to drop out of high school, go to jail, or become teen fathers themselves.

And while no government program can fill the role that fathers play for our children, what we can do is try to support fathers who are willing to step up and fulfill their responsibilities as parents, partners, and providers. That's why last year I started a nationwide dialogue on fatherhood to tackle the challenge of a father's absence head-on.

In Chicago, the Department of Health and Human Services held a forum with community leaders, fatherhood experts, and everyday dads to discuss the importance of responsible fatherhood support programs. In New Hampshire, Secretary of Education Duncan explored the linkages between father absence and educational attainment in children. In Atlanta, Attorney General Holder spoke with

11

fathers in the criminal justice system about ways local reentry organizations, domestic violence groups, and fatherhood programs can join to support ex-offenders and incarcerated individuals who want to be closer to their families and children.

Now we're taking this to the next level. Tomorrow, I'll announce the next phase of our efforts to help fathers fulfill their responsibilities as parents -- The President's Fatherhood and Mentoring Initiative. You can learn more at www.fatherhood.gov.

This Father's Day -- I'm thankful for the opportunity to be a dad to two wonderful daughters. And I'm thankful for all the wonderful fathers, grandfathers, uncles, brothers, and friends who are doing their best to make a difference in the lives of a child.

Happy Father's Day.

Sincerely,

President Barack Obama[3]

Sometimes holding on to your past and not forgiving others will keep you in mental bondage. It may also cause resentment and hostility, which could lead to stress. Spiritual maturity will allow you to *let go* of the past and forgive as God forgives us daily.

---

[3] White House public blog: via the internet.

I was so happy that I forgave my dad. We became best friends before he passed in February 2022. Stay positive, read the Word of God, pray/meditate daily, and always remember, *Change Your Mind & You Change Your Life!*

Who Is Your Role Model?

Thursday: June 17, 2010

Some of us grew up watching cartoon heroes on television and wanted to be like *Superman, Wonder Woman, Spider-Man,* or other famous superheroes today. We may have thought, if I had their strength and power, no one would bother me because I am powerful. We admired these fictional characters as children because they made us feel good about our self-esteem, but mentally safe. We got lost in their world because problems were quickly solved, and there was no *Fear.* Facing reality, they were only fictional characters; not real; their powers were unnatural. Moreover, beneath the fictional characters were people like you and me with real issues.

A role model is someone you look up to and who is worth imitating; someone who can share their difficulties that could help lead you in the right direction; someone who has values, morals, and integrity, and encourages you to do the right things in life.

I always thought of Oprah Winfrey as my earthly role model. She was strong, smart, and courageous, never using her past as an excuse to keep her from her future. Moreover, it allowed her past to give her the strength to fight for her life.

Nevertheless, Jesus is a *perfect* example of a role model in my eyes. He is kind, compassionate, loving, forgiving, and faithful to His word. He is worth imitating. When Jesus walked the earth, He suffered humiliation. He was talked about and mistreated; beaten down because of His undying love for His Father. Yet, through it all, He died for us and took upon Himself the sins of the world. His genuine love: His *agape* love (unconditional love) encourages us daily through the Holy Spirit and the Word of God. Jesus wants us to live a lifestyle pleasing to God of our own free will.

I ask you again, who is your role model? Is it those you see doing evil, making fast money? Or if you are younger, is it someone affiliated with those who go around terrorizing and harassing people by stealing, killing, and being disobedient to their parents to prove independence? Or do you desire the life of the high-paying executive who gets caught up in self-worth? "The thief comes not, but for to steal, and to kill, and to destroy. I am come that they might have life and that they might have it more abundantly (John 10:10)."

These different lifestyles can cut off your days of joy, peace, and eternal life because it is a cruel and selfish way of living; a life not pleasing to God can lead to physical and spiritual death. Being disobedient leads to a negative mindset, which has repercussions: "For the wages of sin is death, but the gift of God is eternal life through Jesus Christ our Lord (Rom. 6:23)."

Are you following God or Satan? Nothing positive will come from following evil. If you do not turn your life around for good, the negative aspect of evil can result in physical and eternal death. I ask again, who is your role model? Is there someone in your life who chooses to follow the right path, which can lead to a godly lifestyle? Think about it! Doing the right things can bring you mental freedom and peace with God. Remember, *Change Your Mind & You Change Your Life!*

Where's Your Armor?

Wednesday: June 16, 2010

Would you go outside without an umbrella or raincoat if it is raining, or a coat if it is freezing? Then why would you leave the house without *The Whole Armor of God?* We know evil exists in our world, and some people do evil things. That is why our government has a military system that always protects us. Moreover, the things we do not see with the natural eye are why we need *The Whole Armor of God,* our spiritual protection. The devil thinks about how he can destroy us daily when he steals our joy and kills our spirit through our minds. "For the weapons of our warfare are not carnal, but mighty through God to the pulling down of strongholds (2 Cor.10:4)." We are in a spiritual war; do not leave home without your protection; put on your armor daily. Not just one or two pieces but *The Whole Armor of God.*

This passage of Ephesians 6 is significant in our daily lives. Please study it and learn to defeat the enemy. This is one of my favorite Scriptures. The devil is trying to take our sanity from us. The best thing we can do is fight back with God's Word. God gives us ammunition, so why not use it daily?

The Whole Armor of God - Ephesians 6:10-20

"Finally, my brethren, be strong in the Lord, and in the power of His might. Put on the whole armour of God, that you may be able to stand against the wiles of the devil. For we do not wrestle against flesh and blood, but against principalities, against powers, against the rulers of the darkness of this world, against spiritual wickedness in the high places. Wherefore take unto you the whole armour of God, that ye may be able to withstand in the evil day, and having done all, to stand. Stand, therefore, having your loins girt about with truth, and having on the breastplate of righteousness; And your feet shod with the preparation of the gospel of peace; Above all, taking the shield of faith, wherewith ye shall be able to quench all the fiery darts of the wicked. And take the helmet of salvation, and the sword of the Spirit, which is the word of God: Praying always with all prayer and supplication in the Spirit, and watching thereunto with all perseverance and supplication for all the saints; And for me, that utterance may be given unto me, that I may open my mouth boldly, to make known the mystery of the gospel, For which I am an ambassador in bonds; that therein I may speak boldly, as I ought to speak."

Again, I say, *Where is Your Armor,* your shield, faith, and protection that God supplies us? Please put on your armor and wear it daily. Keep positive, read the Word, pray/meditate daily, and remember, *Change Your Mind & You Change Your Life!*

16

What You Doin'?

Tuesday: June 15, 2010

What you doin'? How have you all been over the last few days? Is this book helping some to move forward, or are you at a standstill in your life? I hope it is allowing some to move forward. But if you are at a standstill in your life right now, get on your knees and ask God to heal your mind and give you peace that surpasses all understanding. God is a healer and a deliverer if you put your trust in Him. NEVER give up on yourself. The struggle is real, but God is mighty and powerful. The blood of Jesus still works and will never lose its power. When you feel like you are growing tired, weary, or exhausted from everyday life and the obstacles that come, it may seem difficult to pray. So, say the blood of Jesus, and those demons will flee. "Thou believest that there is one God; thou doest well: the devils also believe, and tremble (Jas 2:19)."

When I started this blog, I suggested that everyone take 5-10 minutes daily to pray or meditate. I hope that it has been working out for you. Then I suggested that you get out of the house by doing something you love, like taking a nice walk, treating yourself to dessert, or just doing what relaxes you to get your mind off the busyness of the day. Whatever you like will keep your mind off your worries, which I hope have been a few. Finally, once a month, take a day, a weekend, or even put in for vacation if you have not taken one to enjoy *yourself*. If you cannot take a break right now, there are other ways that are cost-efficient, like a staycation at home without any TVs or phones. If you have children, you may have to send them away to your parents, friends, or daycare; whatever you can do to relax the mind and continue to pray/meditate each day.

We need God daily, no matter what we do or what happens. God is our foundation and strength; "For the joy of the Lord is your strength (Neh. 8:10)." Without God, there is no joy, and without joy, we have no strength. In that case, we need to call on God. We must stand on His Word so that He can be there for us each day, to lift us when we are not feeling our best, and to be there walking in front of us, directing our steps, so we do not stumble and fall. Moreover, to catch us if we do. Remember that God loves you even when you do not love yourself or feel worthy of His love. Continue to pray/meditate daily, read the Word of God, and stay in a positive environment. And remember, *Change Your Mind & You Change Your Life!*

The Truth & Nothing But The Truth

Monday: June 14, 2010

In the courtroom, the judge asked us to place our right hand on the Bible while raising our left hand and proceed to say, Do you swear to tell the *truth*, the whole *truth*, and nothing but the *truth*, so help you, God? They ask you three times if you are going, to be honest. It sounds redundant when you consider how many times they asked the question. The bottom line is that you are either honest or not.

As I have stated many times to friends and family, your word is your bond. Your word is all you have that no one can take from you. When you do not tell the truth, you must continue making more lies to cover the others. Before you know it, you start believing your lies, and the truth becomes void.

There are so many who feel that being honest will hurt them in the long run. And I get it, sometimes when you tell people your deepest thoughts and innermost feelings, it can backfire and be used against you. Especially when you need someone who will not judge or criticize you.

That is why building a relationship with God is important. He will give you discernment and allow you to be able to confide in a trustworthy friend. Someone who is understanding and spiritually knowledgeable. If you do not have anyone that you trust, God is great at listening. "Before they call I will answer; while they are yet speaking I will hear (Isa. 65:24)." God is omniscient, all knowing. Therefore, before you call on Him, He will have an answer to your problems. He is just waiting to hear from you to relieve you of your burdens. If you cannot be honest with people, be honest with God.

We have enough problems without adding fuel to the fire. Honesty is the best policy. It keeps down confusion and builds trust. Lying keeps your mind in bondage mentally and spiritually. "Trust in the LORD with *all* thine heart and lean not unto thine own understanding. In all thy ways acknowledge him, and he shall direct thy paths (Proverbs 3:5-6)."

Put your trust in God, not man, because His Word is truth. "God is not a man, that he should lie; neither the son of man, that he should repent: hath he said, and shall he not do it? Or hath he spoken, and shall he not make it good?" (Numbers 23:19). Be good to yourself, stay positive, and remember, *Change Your Mind & You Change Your Life!*

What Do You Think?

Sunday: June 13, 2010

Some people believe they do not need to read the Bible to succeed in this world. But I pray that you are not one of them. If you choose not to read the Word, you may not receive the faith and strength you need to overcome *fear*. Faith comes by hearing and hearing by the Word of God.

What do you think? Do you think you can live in this world without the knowledge of God? As I stated before, we live in a world full of evil, where the devil is always trying to kill, steal, and destroy whatever God has in store for us, trying to block our blessings. We are in this world but not of the world. We need all the knowledge of God's Word in our minds and hearts to keep strong so that we can persevere even in the face of difficulties. It is impossible to function without God because He is all-powerful. Though through God, all things are possible.

We should be happy for each day that God gives us. "Rejoice always, pray without ceasing, in everything give thanks; for this is the will of God in Christ Jesus for you (1 Thess. 5:16-18)." Each day is a challenge. Whether we go through good or tough times, we must always rejoice in the Lord because all things work together for the good of those who love Him. We cannot lose with the Book we use. What do you think? Stay in His word, pray/meditate, and hold on to a positive attitude each day. And remember, *Change Your Mind & You Change Your Life!*

Passions Of The Flesh

Saturday: June 12, 2010

You have heard the Scripture: 'The Spirit is willing, but the flesh is weak.' The Spirit of God is indeed willing, but it is up to us to say no to the flesh. That is right; we have a choice, free will. The Bible instructs us to watch and pray, not to pray and watch. We are to watch out for evil that comes our way and then pray without ceasing. Each time your flesh wants to do something you know is not of the will of God, pray and ask the Lord to bind that which is evil, and to lose peace and joy, in the name of Jesus. "Watch and pray, lest you enter into temptation. The spirit indeed is willing, but the flesh is weak (Matt: 26:41, NIV)."

People who follow the world's path are likely to obey their sinful nature, not walking according to the Holy Spirit but to the *Passions of the Flesh*. "All of us also lived among them at one time, gratifying the cravings of our sinful nature and following its desires and thoughts. Like the rest, we were by nature objects of wrath (Eph. 2:3, NIV)." Until you get in complete alignment with God, your mind, spirit, and

21

soul, you will have cravings of a sinful fleshly nature that will be hard to deny. Once you are in the will of God, it will be easier for you to say no to your old way of living. Nevertheless, it is your choice.

One illustration is if a doctor tells you to stop smoking because it is harmful to your lungs, and you continue to ignore his advice, which is your flesh, your carnal man, in control. Your fleshly nature or carnal mindedness is not aligned with God's plan for your life. When you submit to the flesh that is because you have not surrendered yourself to the will of the Spirit of God. It is your choice to stop and recognize the sin you are in; drop to your knees and ask God for forgiveness and repent; then roll with Jesus. No one is forcing you to do evil but the *Passions of the Flesh*. Be obedient to God and continue to watch, pray/meditate, and read God's Word. And remember, *Change Your Mind & You Change Your Life!*

Enjoy Life

Friday: June 11, 2010

Life is too short to worry about the things we cannot change. Sometimes we become stressed about everything that goes on in our surrounding environment, and we do not enjoy our surroundings as we desire. For example, watching the sunrise and sunset, or listening to the birds singing beautifully every morning. Do you ever notice how much light the moon gives on the Earth at night? Or consider the planet Venus, which shines so brightly because it is closest to the Sun. All these miracles and signs that God has given us, and we do not notice them. Do you take it for granted when the wind blows, or feel how the breeze brushes past your face? Do you look up and observe how blue the sky is without clouds? When did you last respect the fresh scent of the grass after it rained? Do you note when it rains, how it puts you to sleep peacefully? Do you appreciate how beautiful the flowers are and how the tree brings shade to cool us off from the sun? So much more, I could say. The list goes on and on. However, we only take the time to enjoy the free things in life once something unexpected happens.

There were occasions when I would allow my problems to upset me frequently, until I realized God has always been my Jehovah Jireh, my provider. I started enjoying the things that He has given us. "Therefore, do not worry about tomorrow, for tomorrow will worry about itself. Each day has enough trouble of its own (Matt. 6:34)." Instead of yelling at the kids over spilled milk or because the house is not clean, have a water balloon fight with the kids or play games with them, enjoy life. Walk through the park, get some ice cream, and give God some praise because you are still here, in your right mind, mentally. Enjoy the fun things in life to keep your mind at peace and off negativity. Life is given to us as a *special gift* from God. Please do not take it for granted. Remember, *Change Your Mind & You Change Your Life!*

Do The Right Thing

Thursday: June 10, 2010

We love it when people do things for us to help us out. However, we sometimes hesitate when the circumstances have been reversed and someone needs our help. We often forget this scripture when we

23

become selfish in our daily lives. "So, in everything, *do to others what you would have them do to you*, for this sums up the Law and the Prophets (Matt. 7:12)."

In my daily walk with God, I go through my share of difficulties. Sometimes it gets hard to do the right thing by being kind to others when people mistreat you. But I still do for those who despitefully use me because it is in my spirit to do so. Despite that, if you have the spirit of God in you, you will humble yourself and do the right thing. Humility does not mean to allow others to mistreat you. We must discern how to keep our distance from abusive behavior from others. Nonetheless, become an imitator of Christ to have a clear mind and sleep peacefully at night. Always meditate/pray, enjoy life, and remember, *Change Your Mind & You Change Your Life!*

Do You Have Agape Love For Jesus?

Wednesday: June 9, 2010

This is one of my favorite gospel songs: *"How I Love Jesus" (No One Can Tear Us Apart)* by Pastor Shirley Caesar. There is nothing that God will not do for you. It does not matter what you are going through, God will never leave you. The words to the song are below; whenever you get a chance, listen to her music on YouTube.

> "How I love Jesus, no one can tear us apart; He took my broken pieces and gave me a brand-new start. Have you ever wondered why Jesus loves us so? There are so many tests and trials, but there is one thing I surely know. Sometimes I walk in the valley where trouble meets trouble.

But I can say right now that all my strengths come from the Lord. Now with everything I have left, I am gonna make it last. Giving up the right for the wrong is now a thing of the past. And right now, that I know God words I know the victory is one. I'm so glad that the worst is almost over, and the best is yet to come."[4]

King David was more than just a king; he was a soldier. Being a soldier carries plenty of stress and anxiety. But through it all, King David was a man after God's own heart. *"Because your love is better than life, my lips will glorify you (Psalm 63:3)."* God's love is better than life is a powerful statement. There is no human love that can compare to the *love of God.* Do you love the Lord as much as He loves you? More importantly, can you feel the *love of God?* If not, ask God to pour His love on you, to shower you with all His love. He wants so much to share Himself with you. Invite Him into your life and watch what happens, and witness how much *joy* you will experience.

I love the Lord unconditionally. Nobody can tear us apart. No matter what I have done, God has forgiven me and continues to show His divine love for me daily by continuously showering blessings from heaven on me. To have peace is to have Jesus in your life and to love Him so much that no one can tear you apart from the love of God. It is love that lasts forever. Apostle Paul states in Romans 8:39 that nothing can separate us from God. Continue to pray/meditate daily and remember, *Change Your Mind & You Change Your*

---

[4] Song – *"How I Love Jesus"* by Pastor Shirley Caesar.

Life! Take My Hand

Tuesday: June 8, 2010

The gospel song, *Precious Lord,* has a beautiful meaning.

> "Precious Lord, take my hand, lead me on, and let me stand.
> I am tired, I am weak, and I am worn. Through the storm
> through the night, lead me on to the light. Take my hand,
> precious Lord, and lead me home.

> When my way grows so drear. Oh, precious Lord, I need
> you to linger near. Oh, when my life, blessed life, is over,
> almost gone. Lord, hear my cry. Lord, hear my call. Guide
> my feet lest I fall. Don't let me fall. Take my hand, precious
> Lord, oh Lord. I need you. I need you to guide me hold me
> hide me every step of the way."[5]

Whenever fear tries to come in, I sing the words to this song, *Precious Lord.* I ask God to take my hand and lead me through the storms of life. Like in Psalm 23, "Yea though I walk through the valley of the shadow of death, I will fear no evil, for thou art with me thy rod and thy staff they comfort me." God is always near to comfort us as we walk through the valley. He will protect us by covering us with His feathers and placing a shield around us daily. Look unto the hills from which all my help comes; my help comes from the Lord who made Heaven and Earth. God is the creator of all. He is Alpha and Omega - the beginning and the end – the first and the last. This is

---

[5] Song – *"Take My Hand, Precious Lord"* by Thomas A. Dorsey.

why I love Him so much. "For I, the Lord your God, hold your right hand; it is I who say to you; Fear not, I am the one who helps you (Isa. 41:13)." God will never let go of our hand. He changes not. Do not let go of Him because He will not let go of you. Continue to be encouraged, and remember, *Change Your Mind & You Change Your Life!*

What Direction Are You Going?

Monday: June 7, 2010

Have you ever been so overwhelmed by being pulled in different directions: Paying the bills, doctor appointments, cooking, cleaning, making time for your spouse, taking the children to their events, until you do not know where to start? Just stop and take a deep breath. Before you start your day, ask God, what do you want me to do today? Tell God you have so many things on your agenda that you need Him to order your steps and guide you in the right direction. The Lord gives us the gift of discernment; He is not the author of confusion. "If the LORD delights in a man's way, He makes his *steps firm;* though he stumbles, he will not fall, for the LORD upholds him with His hand (Ps. 37:23-24)."

We have so many seconds, minutes, and hours in a day. If we do not use our time wisely, it will be gone, and we will not enjoy the moments. By now, you should have a schedule as suggested in the *11-step program* to keep organized. If you still need to do so, please take the time to list things you need to do. Remember, procrastination is a sin, and discipline is not enjoyable. "But afterward, there will be a peaceful harvest of right living for those who are trained in this way (Heb. 12:11, NIV)." Training to be disciplined is not easy when going through depression. God is training us to do what is right and not be lazy. However, in the end, when we finish, it will pay off. His Word says we will have a peaceful harvest and live well.

When life's demands begin to weigh heavily and you find yourself at a crossroads, remember that God never intends for you to walk the journey alone. Just as He guides your steps and steadies your heart, He also invites you to pause; breathe, and rely on His wisdom. Trusting in His timing brings order to chaos and clarity to confusion. When you lay your worries at His feet and let go of burdens, you make room for divine direction and peace.

Sometimes, keeping order in daily life feels like walking through a dense fog—uncertainty pressing in from all sides. In those moments, begin prayer and quiet reflection, asking God to clarify the next step, even if He reveals only one at a time. As you move forward in faith, you will find that He gently aligns your priorities and brings purpose to each task, no matter how tedious.

Let your actions be an outpouring of trust in Him, for His faithfulness never fails. Each small choice, each moment surrendered, strengthens the foundation of your character and shapes the legacy you leave behind. In seeking His will above your own, you work not just discipline but also enduring joy—a peace that persists beyond circumstances.

Therefore, God will be there for you to direct your path, creating less stress and more time to meditate/pray, reflect, and enjoy your day. He will be there to uphold you with His hand, so you will not fall. However, if you fall, He will catch you. God loves you unconditionally and will never leave you or forsake you. Always think positive thoughts and remember, *Change Your Mind & You Change Your Life!*

Action Speaks Louder Than Words

Sunday: June 6, 2010

You've heard the phrase; action speaks louder than words. Well, that is true. It is not always what you say, but what you do, that people pay more attention to. What are your values? What makes you do the things that you do in life? Are your morals aligning with the Word so that your children want to be like you? Do you have integrity? Are you an excellent example to your children and your community, where people want to hear what you say, or do they turn and walk in a different direction when they see you coming? Do your actions make you stress more? Does your action speak louder than your words? If you have integrity, you will experience peace knowing that you have done right in the sight of God. "The man of integrity walks securely, but he who takes crooked paths will be found out (Proverbs 10:9)."

No matter how much you try to deceive people by what you say, your actions will speak for you. Your word is your bond. When you say things you do not mean, people lose confidence in you, which can cause people not to trust you. Knowing this can bring on unwanted stress and make you feel empty inside. It shows a side of doublemindedness and not being stable. When others know they can count on you, it can also eliminate their stress. But most of all, they learn to trust in you. Have you ever known someone that you knew you could not trust? No matter what promises they make, you always doubt them. Do you want to be like this?

That is why God's Word is true. He wants you to trust and test Him. Know that He is God and does not lie. "So, shall my word be that goeth forth out of my mouth: it shall not return unto me void, but it shall accomplish that which I please, and it shall prosper in the thing whereto I sent it (Isaiah 55:11)." Let your actions justify your integrity and walk securely for the Lord by living the lifestyle of Christ. When people believe in you, they will believe in what you stand for, which is the Word of God. Be a doer of the word, and if you cannot be honest; with people, be honest with God by meditating and praying. And remember, *Change Your Mind & You Change Your Life!*

Take Care Of Your Body

Saturday: June 5, 2010

Have you heard the saying You are what you eat? You might not be physically what you eat, but what goes into your body has plenty to do with your health. Sometimes we eat when we are stressed out, upset, or depressed. We often do not pay attention to how much we eat and end up overweight, causing high blood pressure, diabetes, etc. It is not just how much you eat but what you are eating. "Whether you eat or drink or whatever you do, do it all for the glory of God (1 Cor. 10:31)."

God does not want us to eat foods we know are bad for us. I love junk food, but overindulging is not healthy. Harming your body is not glorifying God. I always say you eat to live, not live to eat. I used to binge on chocolates and plenty of salty foods, which took a toll on my body. When I was younger, I gained 30 pounds and two dress sizes due to excessive stress and overeating. I was at a crossroads where I could not lose this weight on my own, so I joined *Weight Watchers*[6]. I am glad I made that choice. *Weight Watchers* taught me how to eat whatever I wanted in moderation. *Weight Watchers* also taught me to respect and enjoy the food I desired without worrying about overeating.

Life challenges can present stress. Trying to learn your body's triggers while doing this is helpful. Next time, figure out what triggered you to eat more. Eating healthy foods and drinking water will help you the next time a stressful situation triggers you. This can also help reduce weight gain. You should write down your stress triggers and work on solutions to your problems.

Reminder: In the beginning, I told you to take 5-10 minutes to meditate/pray daily. Hope you are obedient. When you are anxious,

---

[6] Weight Watchers, www.weightwatchers.com. Weight Watchers is *the* #1 doctor-recommended weight-loss program†. Additionally, our diabetes-tailored plan is based on guidelines from the American Diabetes Association and the International Diabetes Federation.

taking five minutes to relax will help calm you and give you mental freedom. Give your problems to the Lord, who will work them out for you. You may say it is easier said than done. However, everything takes time and practice. Being consistent in your praying and reading your word is the key to changing the way you think.

Take your burdens to the Lord and leave them there. Jesus will fix your problems. "Cast thy burden upon the LORD, and He shall sustain thee: He shall never suffer the righteous to be moved (Ps. 55:22)." After all, He is a problem solver. God wants you to care for your mind, body, and soul so you can do His will. If you do not take care of yourself, then who will? Ask God to help comfort you and give you the strength you need to make it each day. Keep the *Now* faith and trust in God for all your needs. Remember, *Change Your Mind & You Change Your Life!*

Sweet Sleep

Friday: June 4, 2010

Sleep is essential to our bodies, just like food and water. Not having adequate rest can make you feel tired, grouchy, and sometimes irritable when you do not get enough sleep. Proper rest to restore our bodies is essential in dealing with everyday stress. Not getting the right amount of sleep increases stress and can make you less able to deal with stressful situations. Even minor problems, without sufficient relaxation, your body could suffer exhaustion. As adults, the body requires at least 7-9 hours of restful, peaceful sleep, which I call *sweet sleep*. This means you sleep so peacefully that nothing disturbs you through the night, not even dreaming.

Sometimes it is hard to sleep because of tense situations that may arise, and our minds are not at ease. Dreaming about your issues is not getting adequate rest. I call myself a dream child. I did not realize that dreaming is not resting, and I would wake up tired. (*Contact your physician if you are having problems sleeping*.) We need to have peace of mind that will allow us to sleep peacefully through the night. "I will lie down and sleep in peace, for you alone, O LORD, make me dwell in safety" (Psalm 4:8). It is easy to rest when you do not have problems. Yet, God will keep your mind at peace if your mind stays on Him. "When you lie down, you will not be afraid; when you lie down, your *sleep will be sweet* (Proverbs 3:24)." When I found it difficult to sleep, reading the Bible became an excellent sleeping pill. Continue to meditate/pray each day. Stay positive, and remember, *Change Your Mind & You Change Your Life!*

How Solid Is Your Foundation?

Thursday: June 3, 2010

Working in construction for many years, I found out that before you can build a house or a building, you must make sure the foundation is solid. You cannot build upon sand because it is not a firm foundation. You must build on solid rock. Our life is just like a building. We need a solid foundation, which is our spiritual awareness, to stand firm. We must build on Jesus' blood and righteousness. He is our solid rock, which consists of meditating/praying and reading the Word each day. "And I say also unto thee, that thou art Peter, and upon this rock, I will build my church; and the gates of hell shall not prevail against it (Matt. 16:18)." In having a solid foundation, thou strongholds may come, the building may shake but not fall.

You must have a personal relationship with God to hear His voice and understand God's plan for your life. "But the one who hears my words and does not put them into practice is like a man who built a house on the ground without a foundation. The moment the torrent struck that house, it collapsed, and its destruction was complete (Luke 6:49, NIV)." The enemy constantly attempts in every way possible to prevent us from staying strong in the Lord. The Word says to pray without ceasing. This does not mean nonstop, but it means constantly recurring, being consistent.

Apostle Paul went through temptations and struggles; he knew to call on Jesus as soon as issues arose. You should not take your time like the woman with the issue of blood who waited 12 long years before she went to Christ. Not only did she go through some rough spots in her life, but she also asked everyone for help, but God. Trying to fix or solve a problem on our own never ends the way we want it to. And not having a solid foundation, not believing, and not trusting in God can lead us to various temptations as well. We may not want to do wrong, but if we are not fully connected to Christ, our carnal man will rise without hesitation. Apostle Paul said it best:

> "For that which I do, I allow not; for what I would, that do I not; but what I hate, that do I. If then I do that which I would not, I consent unto the law that it is good. Now then

it is no more I that do it, but sin that dwelleth in me. For I know that in me (that is, in my flesh,) dwelleth no good thing: For to will is present with me; but how to perform that which is good I find not. For the good that I would I do not: but the evil which I would not, that I do. Now if I do that I would not, it is no more I that do it, but sin that dwelleth in me. I find then a law, that, when I would do good, evil is present with me (Romans 7:15-21)."

Evil is constantly trying to steal your joy. We must constantly pray/meditate without ceasing. Secure your foundation by delighting in God's law and allow Him to be the cornerstone. Remember, *Change Your Mind & You Change Your Life!*

The Stressed & The Restless

Wednesday: June 2, 2010

There are good days and bad days that we must encounter daily. However, it is how we handle situations that determines how we feel later. There were times when I spoke with my mom, and she became overwhelmed with concerns about what was happening in the world. I try to comfort her and reassure her that God sees all, telling her to try to relax and enjoy life. But her compassion for others caused anxiety. Then I told her there is only so much we can do as individuals to help people. It also takes a multitude of people on one accord to change things. "And when the day of Pentecost was fully come they were *all* with *one accord* in one place. And *suddenly* there came a sound from heaven as of a rushing mighty wind, and it filled all the house where they were sitting (Acts 2:1-2)." The Disciples and others who were waiting for Jesus' instructions in the Upper Room were not stressed or restless. They spent their time fasting and praying, waiting to hear from God. Being surrounded by like-minded people makes a difference in the atmosphere.

Nevertheless, being around others who are stressed can also trigger stress factors. When my mom was stressing out, I sometimes allowed it to upset me, and now the *transfer of emotions* is causing me anxiety. Then there are my children, whom I love dearly, who take life as though it were a chess game, waiting for their next turn to move on, not knowing what needs to be done, which should be getting life in order. I spend time worrying about them because they have spouses and children. I know I should not let it pressure me, but I do. Here it is again; the stress of restlessness transferring onto me. Some people say that is what young adults do at their age. However, being a mother can be difficult, watching them make mistakes.

Stress can lead to restlessness and tiredness; That being fatigued all the time is not what God wants for us. This goes back to one of my blogs about getting your house in order. I am not perfect. However, I know that living stress-free can be difficult at times. But I never give up trying. I enforced rules in my house to get the kind of peace I needed with my children, which sometimes led to unhappy faces. As for my mother, we used to pray together, which took our minds off the problem and onto the problem solver, Jehovah Jireh. It is not the problems we have, it is how to deal with them. "Oh, that I had the wings of a dove! I would fly away and be at rest. I would flee far away and stay in the desert; Selah (Ps. 55:6-7)." We all feel like this sometimes if we could fly away to peace and rest. God will give us peace of mind if we meditate/pray each day and stay away from negative people. He is our dessert. Continue to walk in the Lord and remember, *Change Your Mind & You Change Your Life.*

Keep Your Eye On The Real Prize

Tuesday: June 1, 2010

When I was a little girl, I loved eating Cracker Jacks. The fun part was waiting to get the prize at the bottom of the box. After I found the prize, it was not what I wanted, so I went back to the store the next day and got another box. Sometimes the prize was fun, but most of the time it was boring. Either way, I did not gain anything from it one way or the other. That is how we are when we go to the fair and win prizes, we spend endless time and money to get the biggest stuffed animal we can. And after we get it, the thrill is gone.

We should keep our eye on the real prize! The prize that lasts forever, for a lifetime, for eternity. This prize is not boring but brings joy and life to all who obtain it.

1 Cor. 9:24-27, NIV

"Do you not know that in a race all the runners run, but only one gets the prize? Run in such a way as to get the prize. Everyone who competes in the games goes into strict training. They do it to get a crown that will not last, but we do it to get a crown that will last forever. Therefore, I do not

37

run like a man running aimlessly; I do not fight like a man beating the air. No, I strike a blow to my body and make it my slave so that after I have preached to others, I, myself will not be disqualified for the prize."

So, are you like runners who spend their time getting their bodies into shape, knowing that only one person will win the gold, competing only for self-gratification? Or do you want to spend your time and energy preaching the word of God, knowing for sure that you are certainly going to get the gold, doing the will of God, not for yourself but to please God?

In this race, everyone who keeps their eye on the prize of the high calling of God will get a *Crown* that will last forever. I say keep your eye on the real prize, which will bring everlasting peace. Never lose sight of where you are headed. Jesus never took his eye off God. The Lord never became distracted but stayed focused on God's plan for His life. That is the real prize. So, stay positive, keep your eye on the real prize, and remember, *Change Your Mind & You Change Your Life!*

A Good Fight

Monday: May 31, 2010

First, I would like to say I hope everyone enjoyed a beautiful Memorial Day. And my heart goes out to all the fallen soldiers, those soldiers who fought in the past as well as the soldiers fighting and protecting us today. Without the military protecting us, we would be lost. You are truly blessed and highly favored for your patriotism.

Like our soldiers, are you giving your all to your cause? Are you putting up a good fight, striving to keep your mind at peace? You must continue to fight a good fight when it comes to deleting stress. Continue to stay positive and relax for at least 30 minutes to one hour a day. Just take a few minutes to relax your mind. Just lay back, lift your feet, and enjoy some soft music. Smooth jazz is my favorite music that relaxes me. Only you know what helps you to relax.

Sometimes we must fight for what we want. And if you want peace, you must fight for it daily by praying, meditating without ceasing, and reading the word. "Therefore, I urge you, brothers, in view of God's mercy, to offer your bodies as living sacrifices, holy and pleasing to God—this is your spiritual act of worship. Do not conform any longer to the pattern of this world but be transformed by the _renewing of your mind._ Then you will be able to test and approve what God's will is—His good, pleasing, and perfect will (Romans 12:1-2, NIV)."

To fight a good fight, you must _renew_ your mind, so you can think for yourself; be in control of everything around you. The devil wants you to lose control over your mind, to be out of control. Your mind is the gateway to your entire being. Continue to keep up the good fight with the help of the Lord. He will always be there when you want Him if you call upon His name, JESUS, the name that is sweeter than a honeycomb. Remember to eat healthily and keep positive thoughts. And do not forget, _Change Your Mind & You Change Your Life!_

Laborers For Hire

Sunday: May 30, 2010

Do you want to work or just do nothing for the rest of your life? Do you want to live off other people's fortune and hard work or be a laborer for the Lord? "Jesus went through all the towns and villages, teaching in their synagogues, preaching the good news of the kingdom, and healing every disease and sickness. When he saw the crowds, he had compassion for them, because they were harassed and helpless, like sheep without a shepherd. Then he said to his disciples, The harvest is plentiful, but workers are few (Matt. 9:35-38, NIV)."

Ask the Lord of the harvest, therefore, to send out workers into his harvest field. Jesus told his disciples that there are so many souls that need deliverance and healing, but there are not enough workers for the kingdom of God wanting to work for Christ to help teach, heal, and lead people to do the will of God. Spreading the Word of God should be joyful, a pleasure, and a fulfilling job. You should be honored to be a Laborer for the Lord. Not treating it as a chore. I am very blessed that God has called and chosen me to do His will. Each time I can minister to someone, I delight myself to do so. It makes my spirit feel so good because I know the Lord is pleased. I know that the angels in heaven are rejoicing along with me because my spirit rejoices when I say the name of Jesus. Be a laborer for the Lord and work His harvest so that it will bring joy to your heart and peace to your mind. Remember, *Change Your Mind & You Change Your Life!*

Motivation

Saturday: May 29, 2010

One thing I experienced while depressed, was my desire to stay motivated. You may ask yourself, why should I go on because no one cares. You feel lonely and worthless, as if it is not effective what you are doing. On the other hand, doing nothing is going to make you feel worse.

God does not want you to feel sorry for yourself. Therefore, pray and ask God to help you get motivated; to lift your spirit by filling you with His love, peace, and grace. Ask Him to cover you with His feathers and hide you under His wings to protect you from evil and to bring joy into your heart and soul by guarding your mind.

We must give ourselves *completely* to the Lord. "Therefore, my dear brothers, stand firm. Let nothing move you. Always give yourselves fully unto the Lord, because you know that your labor in the Lord is not in vain (1 Cor. 15:58, NIV)." When you give yourself fully to the Lord, you will be able to do exceedingly above and beyond all human expectations. And your work in the Lord will not go unnoticed. God knows our struggles, and He will never leave us alone to deal with them ourselves. Just leave it in the hands of the Lord, and He will show up and show out, if we just ask.

Get up from that couch, out of bed and do the work of the Lord. God wants us at our best so we can defeat the enemy. Take care of yourself physically and mentally. Go out and buy some clothes and give yourself a makeover or even take a mini vacation to your favorite weekend hideaway so you can relax. Not only will this make you feel great, but you will be highly motivated to do the work of the Lord. Remember, *Change Your Mind & You Change Your Life!*

You Talkin' About Me!

Friday, May 28, 2010

You have heard the expression, the pot calling the kettle black. "Do not judge, and you will not be judged. Do not condemn, and you will not be condemned. Forgive, and you will be forgiven. Give and it will be given to you. A good measure, pressed down, shaken together, and running over, will be poured into your lap. For with the measure you use, it will be measured to you (Luke 6:37-38, NIV)."

Many times, we judge others by what others say without knowing the facts. We can easily see other people's mistakes more than we see our own. It is easier to point the finger at someone else instead of giving good advice or ministering to them. We should never judge others for their wrongdoing because God never condemns us for ours. Just like He forgives us, we should forgive others. It may be difficult sometimes to forgive those who use you, abuse you, talk about you, or mistreat you. Our hearts become hardened and therefore we block some of the blessings of God.

When you forgive, God will forgive you for all your mistakes. When you give kindness, love, and compassion it will come back to you. We often feel stressed and worried when we have misunderstandings with our loved ones. Communication becomes distant because no one wants to be the bigger person and apologize. Life is too short to be tenacious. Everyone makes mistakes and says things they do not mean out of hurt and pain. However, we know that God is love and we need the love of God in our hearts to speak good toward one another.

Praying for those who have hurt you and for yourself to be able to forgive, will bring you closer to God. Forgive them and move on with your life. You will feel stress-free and happier in the days to come. Forgiveness is not for them so much as it is for you to receive. "But if ye forgive not men their trespasses, neither will your Father forgive your trespasses (Matt. 6:14-15)." This passage of scripture touched my heart when it comes to forgiving others. When I thought about God not forgiving me each time I pray for my wrongdoings because I would not forgive others was critical not only to my soul but to my eternal life.

It is a hard pill to swallow when we have been hurt many times. We must *renew* our minds by thinking more like Christ. After all, peace of mind is far better than having anxiety of the soul. Continue to pray/meditate, have a good attitude, forgive, and remember, *Change Your Mind & You Change Your Life!*

Children, I'm Home!

Wednesday: May 26, 2010

When we were young, my grandparents used to leave my oldest sister and I in charge. We would have a couple of friends over and have a ball not knowing when my grandparents would come home. But we always managed to get everything back in order before they arrived. Then there were times the house was not in order because time had flown by and before you knew it we had to clean up quickly as possible with some chores left unfinished. There was a huge price to pay if you know what I mean. It is the same with God. We do not know the day or the hour that Jesus will come to take us home. We must always be on guard and alert; meaning to always carry the spirit of God wherever we go.

> "No one knows about that day or hour, not even the angels in heaven, nor the Son, but only the Father. Be on guard! Be alert! You do not know when that time will come. It's like a man going away: He leaves his house and puts his servants in charge, each with his assigned task, and tells the one at the door to keep watch. Therefore, keep watch because you do not know when the owner of the house will come back—whether in the evening, or at midnight, or when the rooster crows, or at dawn. If he comes suddenly, do not let him find you sleeping. What I say to you, I say to everyone: Watch! (Mk. 13:32-37)"

You should always do what is pleasing to God by keeping your house in order and living a righteous lifestyle. Living in obedience will keep you at peace and right standing until Jesus returns. Always, pray/meditate daily and remember, *Change Your Mind & You Change Your Life!*

Love Your Enemies

Thursday: May 27, 2010

I know I keep emphasizing the word *Love*. However, there is so much hate and crime in the world today everyone is forgetting about God. God is *Love*. "But I say to you who hear [Me and pay attention to My words]: **Love** [that is, unselfishly seek the best or higher good for] **your enemies**, [make it a practice to] do good to those who hate you, bless and show kindness to those who curse you, **pray** for those who mistreat you (Luke 6:27-28, AMP)." The heart of Jesus teaches *Love*. Jesus commands that we *Love* everyone even our enemies. Striving for perfection in Christ should be our example and goal; to be perfect in being more like Jesus. If everybody were like Jesus what a wonderful world this would be. Imagine living in a world where there is only peace. So, give a little kindness, give a little *love*, show some compassion, mercy, and remember, *Change Your Mind & You Change Your Life!*

Practice What You Preach

Tuesday: May 25, 2010

Many times, we can tell others what to do but when it comes to taking our own advice, sometimes we fall short. For example, it is easy for us to criticize people on how they spend their money, but we rob God of tithes and offerings. "Will a man rob God? Yet ye have robbed me. But ye say, Wherein have we robbed thee? In tithes and offerings (Malachi 3:8)." We can gossip about the friend who did not pay you back the money you loaned them. Then we are afraid to answer the

45

phone when a bill collector calls. It is easy to talk about people who smoke, drink, and do drugs but you curse your children and call them names when they make mistakes. This list can go on and on.

Giving our tithes and offering is the first phase to obtaining peace. How is that possible you may ask? I am living proof of having faith in believing that I cannot beat God giving, which brings peace to my spirit. The more I give the more He gives to me. I do not give to receive; I give because I am obedient to the Word of God. And because I love God with my entire being.

I was not always this way when it came to giving 10% of tithes. The less I gave God the more stressed I became when paying bills. It felt like I had a hole in my pocket. Sometimes, we put ourselves in a financial bind, then deny God what is His. However, we manage to give to the world system by spending all our money on things we want and do not need. But when it comes to getting back from the world system, you must have A-one credit. God does not care about your credit; He cares about your love for Him and your obedience to His Word.

When I decided to put my trust in God, not only did I feel better, but my bills started to decrease, and the blessings of the Lord started to increase. We were not created to stress and have anxiety but to praise and worship the Lord. "Worship the LORD with gladness; come before him with joyful songs (Ps. 100:2)." Now I practice what I preach. Give and it shall be given to you. What is given to me, peace of mind. Then Jesus said to the crowds and his disciples: "The teachers of the law and the Pharisees sit in Moses' seat. So, you must obey them and do everything they tell you. But do not do what they do, for they do not practice what they preach. They tie up heavy loads and put them on men's shoulders, but they themselves are not willing to lift a finger to move them (Matt. 23:1-4)."

Before we can judge others we should do like the song that the late Michael Jackson wrote: Look at *The Man in The* Mirror. Correct your ways and follow Christ. *Practice what you preach.* Keep a positive attitude, treat people with kindness, and remember, *Change Your Mind & You Change Your Life!*

The Greatest Commandment

Monday: May 24, 2010

What is the greatest commandment in the bible? Some of you may be thinking hard right now. But if you would sum up the bible in its entirety and think about what would make the world a better place then you could answer this question sincerely. Or should I say, what does God represent to you? If you answered *love,* then you are truly right. God is *love.* The entire Bible teaches about *love.* The answer is below:

> "Hearing that Jesus had silenced the Sadducees, the Pharisees got together. One of them, an expert in the law, tested him with this question: "Teacher, which is the greatest commandment in the Law?" Jesus replied: Love the Lord your God with all your heart and with all your soul and with all your mind. This is the first and greatest commandment. And the second is like it: Love your

47

neighbor as yourself. All the Law and the Prophets hang on these two commandments (Matt. 22:34-40, NIV)."

To *love* God with all your heart, all your soul, all your mind, and all your strength, is the first and greatest commandment. You know what is in my heart at this moment? That God should not have had to make this a command. Because of His grace, goodness, and mercy, we should *love* God anyway. I do not know about you, but I *love* God because of who He is not because of everything that He has done for me and my family. I love Him for allowing me to see another day, for putting food on my table, for providing shelter, for keeping me in good health, for forgiving me when I do wrong, and for showing me unconditional love. Why wouldn't I Love God with all my heart, soul, mind, and strength? He is so good to me and favors me highly.

God does not command us to love Him because of His power to do so. We were designed to be in relationship with Him. It is not an option. For example, if we do not brush our teeth, they would fall out. Other words, God loves us unconditionally, so it is just for us to love Him. How can we not love a God who created us in His image. Moreover, how can we love others if we cannot love Him?

Love your neighbor as yourself can be an exceedingly difficult commandment, especially when people mistreat us. However, it is the second and greatest commandment. Loving someone who hurts you and uses you is quite difficult at times. Nevertheless, I have learned to love those who despitefully use me. I know you think she is just saying that because of my status as a woman of God. Trust me, I am not. It was difficult for me, especially as a child. I would get disciplined because I did not like apologizing. I truly meant the negative things I used to say or how I mistreated people because of how I was mistreated. The person I used to be would just do unto others and not feel any compassion; having a bad attitude towards those who did me wrong; not forgiving or speaking to people for years at a time without compunction. Then I realized that God forgave me when I was a backslider. He forgave me when I used to curse and party all night. And when I had all *three* of my children out of wedlock. God loved me when I did not love myself. Then I realized if He could forgive me for not taking the time out to praise Him every day or to pray except for when I needed something, then I can surely love my neighbor as God loves me.

Think about it. Who am I to not want to have a forgiving nature, when I am a follower of Christ? We are not perfect. So why mistreat others when we have faults of our own? God is *love*. And to love God is to love everyone. Remember, *Change Your Mind & You Change Your Life!*

I'm Not A Hypocrite: Am I!

Sunday: May 23, 2010

When you do virtuous deeds for those who are in need, do you do it with a crowd around or in private? Do you brag about how much you do for others or boast about how much you donate to charities or how much you give in offerings in church? If so, you are a hypocrite, a showoff, a pretender, play-acting.

Matthew 6:3-5

"But when you give to the needy, do not let your left hand know what your right hand is doing, so that your giving may be in secret. Then your Father, who sees what is done in secret, will reward you. "And when you pray, do not be like the **hypocrites,** for they love to pray standing in the synagogues and on the street corners to be seen by men. I tell you the truth, they have received their reward in full."

Matthew 23:13-15

"But woe unto you, scribes and Pharisees, **hypocrites!** for ye shut up the kingdom of heaven against men: for ye neither go in yourselves, neither suffer ye them that are entering to go in. Woe unto you, scribes and Pharisees, **hypocrites!** for ye devour widows' houses, and for a pretense make long prayer: therefore, ye shall receive the greater damnation. Woe unto you, scribes and Pharisees, **hypocrites!** For ye compass sea and land to make one proselyte, and when he is made, ye make him twofold more the child of hell than yourselves."

God loves a cheerful giver. Give from your heart because you want to give. You do not have to impress anyone. The only one who matters is God and He sees everything that you do and knows why you are doing it. God seeks the heart and mind of man. Give because you want to and not in expectation. Stop trying to impress humanity and be a God-pleaser. What charitable deeds are done in the dark, God will reward openly. Therefore, stay kind, positive and spread some cheer, and remember, *Change Your Mind & Change Your Life!*

What Is Your Goal?

Saturday: May 22, 2010

What are your goals in life? Do you spend time in the past or are you pressing on toward the future? Many of us spend so much time in self-pity about the mistakes we have made when the future holds so much more. We must press toward the goal; not our goal; but the goal of Christ. "Not that I have already obtained all this, or have already been made perfect, but I press on to take hold of that for which Christ Jesus took hold of me. Brothers, I do not consider myself yet to have taken hold of it. But one thing I do: Forgetting what is behind and straining toward what is ahead, I press on toward the goal to win the prize for which God has called me heavenward in Christ Jesus (Phil. 3:12-15, NIV)." All of us who are spiritually mature should take such a view of things. Moreover, at some point you think differently that God will make all things clear to you.

We must look at our past not as mistakes, but as an *experience* we needed to obtain wisdom and knowledge for future lessons. Then move on to what God has in store for us, which is to take hold of that for which Christ Jesus took hold of me. Which means Christ will supply all your needs. You must move forward. However, do not forget the past, but leave it behind as a stepping stool and a learning tool. Aim high toward the prize, which is salvation and righteousness. Our ultimate aspirations are found not in this life but in heaven because Jesus is there.

We need to make more progress in our spiritual growth and stability so we can press on toward our goals. So, keep meditating/praying and staying positive, and remember, *Change Your Mind & You Change Your Life!*

Where Does Your Help Come From?

Friday: May 21, 2010

There comes a time in everyone's life when they may need the assistance of someone. We all need someone at some time in our life. When I need help I turn to the passage below and read it loudly. I know my help comes from the Lord.

Psalm 121

"I lift up my eyes to the hills—where does my help come from? My help comes from the LORD, the Maker of heaven and earth. He will not let your foot slip—he who watches over you will not slumber; indeed, He who watches over Israel will neither slumber nor sleep. The LORD watches over you—the LORD is your shade at your right hand; the sun will not harm you by day, nor the moon by night. The LORD will keep you from all harm—He will watch over your life; the LORD will watch over your coming and going both now and forevermore."

I have been in some tight situations wondering how I am going to make it out when I have done everything humanly possible. Then God steps in and shows out. He is the King of all creations, so I know I am in good hands. His assurance is in verse four concerning the

52

unsleeping guardian over Israel. Rest assured that He is our guardian as well. Even when the way is treacherous; He does not slumber. He is the One in whom the faithful may put unfaltering trust assuring unfailing protection. For all that distresses or threatens us day or night, God will be our shade our protector from all evil concerning life. The Lord will watch over our coming and going both now and forevermore. Just put your trust in the Lord and He will always be there for you. The next time you need help, lift up your eyes to the hills. Stay positive and remember, *Change Your Mind & You Change Your Life!*

Blessings From God

Thursday: May 20, 2010

To be blessed by God is to have favor. Read the scripture below and count your blessings. Read Deuteronomy for blessings regarding being obedient to God.

Deuteronomy 28:1-14

"If you fully obey the LORD your God and carefully follow all his commands I give you today, the LORD your God will set you high above all the nations on earth. All these blessings will come upon you and accompany you if you obey the LORD your God: You will be blessed in the city and blessed in the country. The fruit of your womb will be blessed, and the crops of your land and the young of your livestock—the calves of your herds and the lambs of your flocks. Your basket and your kneading trough will be

53

blessed. You will be blessed when you come in and blessed when you go out. The LORD will grant that the enemies who rise up against you will be defeated before you. They will come at you from one direction but flee from you in seven. The LORD will send a blessing on your barns and on everything you put your hand to. The LORD your God will bless you in the land he is giving you. The LORD will establish you as his holy people, as he promised you on oath if you keep the commands of the LORD your God and walk in his ways. Then all the peoples on earth will see that you are called by the name of the LORD, and they will fear you. The LORD will grant you abundant prosperity—in the fruit of your womb, the young of your livestock, and the crops of your ground—in the land he swore to your forefathers to give you. The LORD will open the heavens, the storehouse of his bounty, to send rain on your land in season and to bless all the work of your hands. You will lend to many nations but will borrow from none. The LORD will make you the head, not the tail. If you pay attention to the commands of the LORD your God that I give you this day and carefully follow them, you will always be at the top, never at the bottom. Do not turn aside from any of the commands I give you today, to the right or to the left, following other gods and serving them."

Stay blessed and remember, *Change Your Mind & You Change Your Life!*

Are You Obedient?

Wednesday: May 19, 2010

Are you obedient to the Word of God? Are you a follower or a leader? Do you want to do the right thing? We all try to do the best that we can to please the Lord; I know I try extremely hard. But like Paul said, "Every time I desire to do good evil is always present." That's why we must pray and stay in God's word daily.

It is very easy to be tempted to do wrong. Afterall, it started in the Garden of Eden with His creation. Satan was there cunning and deceiving Adam and Eve with the playing of words. "You will not surely die (Genesis 3:4)." They did not die right away; however, their spirit separated from God. The first thing was separation, spiritual death; then natural death. Mankind was created to live here on earth forever. That is why when we are disobedient to doing God's will, we feel distant. I want to tell you that we are never alone. We just feel lonely because we have not confessed our sins to Him and repented.

Read the book of Deuteronomy 27 & 28:15-68, so that you may understand what God is saying regarding obedience. Obedience comes with blessings. Therefore, stay positive, be obedient, and remember, *Change Your Mind & You Change Your **Life!***

Peaceful Thinking

Tuesday: May 18, 2010

Many times, we wake up to the same problems. But this day I woke up with my mind stayed on Jesus. It is not easy trying to keep your mind together with all the worries and issues we face today. Especially with the economy, health, and personal problems we face daily. Take it from me I know how that feels. But we must renew our minds by reading the Bible each day and meditating and praying constantly. Remembering scriptures is good training for the mind. It takes your mind of the negativity that may surround you and put you in a positive realm. If you do not get a chance to read your bible before leaving the house, you can think about Scriptures you memorized throughout the day.

One of my favorites is Psalm 23. It keeps me peaceful throughout the day. You too will find a scripture you will learn that takes your mind off negative thoughts and brings you into tranquility.

Romans 12:1-2

> "Therefore, I urge you, brothers, in view of God's mercy, to offer your bodies as living sacrifices, holy and pleasing to God—this is your spiritual act of worship. **2** Do not conform any longer to the pattern of this world but be transformed by the **renewing of your mind**. Then you will be able to test and approve what God's will is—his good, pleasing, and perfect will."

Renew your mind by watching positive movies on television, being around positive people, listening to spiritual music or music that is pleasant and soothing to the mind. It is especially important to have a positive and peaceful environment. During these things can help change the way you think and help you make better choices in the things that you do. Speaking positive words promotes relaxation, peace, joy, happiness, inspires hope, help with the recovery process of healing, boosts your self-esteem and drives motivation. Overall, it will give empowerment to your daily life. Therefore, go to sleep thinking pleasant thoughts and you will wake up thinking pleasant thoughts, even more if you allow the Word of God to penetrate in your mind.

If any of you have been through surgery, you know they give you anesthesia. Whatever you are talking about and how you feel before you go under is how you will feel when you wake up. When I had surgery, I was laughing as I fell asleep and when I woke up I was laughing. *Get the picture?* Just stay positive and your life will be much better. And remember, *Change Your Mind & You Change Your Life!*

My House

Monday: May 17, 2010

What is going on in your house? Is it pleasant or noisy with confusion or is it filled with laughter? Do you thank God for your meals or just eat without praying? Do you wake up and go about your daily tasks without asking God to build a wall of protection around you? Moreover, do you take a shower then watch a little television before you fall asleep without praying to God to take your soul if you should die during the night?

Joshua 24:15

"But if serving the LORD seems undesirable to you, then choose for yourselves this day whom you will serve, whether the gods your forefathers served beyond the River or the gods of the Amorites, in whose land you are living. But as for **me and my household**, we will serve the LORD."

Choose you this day whom you and your family will serve. Will you serve God in *your house* that you might have peace and order? Or will you continue to have chaos and havoc and be depressed because of your children not being obedient or your spouse not acting accordingly? It should not even be an option! I choose to serve God in *My House*. Keep positive and remember, *Change Your Mind & You Change Your Life!*

What's In Your Spirit?

Saturday: May 15, 2010

Are you depressed, worried, or fearful? And your spirit is not what it used to be, finding yourself with no pep in your step. Moreover, there is no laughter or smiles left inside you. You just cannot seem to shake what is bothering you no matter how hard you try. The Lord says in the scripture below that God is close to the brokenhearted and delivers you from trouble.

Psalm 34:18-19

"The LORD is close to the brokenhearted and saves those who are crushed in spirit. A righteous man may have many

58

troubles, but the LORD delivers him from them all."

So, when you are feeling down just read God's word. The entire chapter of Psalm 34 is a delightful book to read. Then meditate and pray, asking God to remove all your heaviness from your spirit. As I stated earlier, Psalm 23 is one of my favorite books of the bible. When it says, *"Your rod and your staff, they comfort me."* Thy rod and staff represent guidance, protection, and care. And comfort means that God has the power to give you peace during your trials and tribulation. Therefore, ask God to comfort you in times of trouble and He will. God loves you and does not want you to be unhappy. Your ship will finally come if you trust in the Lord always.

Without further delay, get back into the swing of things with a great big smile. Also, uplift someone with a kind word who just may be feeling the same way. You never know whose spirit is broken and just might need a kind word or two spoken to them. Stay uplifting and motivated. Do not complain just enjoy the beauty of the Lord. And remember, *Change Your Mind & You Change Your Life!*

In The Midst

Sunday: May 16, 2010

When you are going through trials and tribulations call on Jesus and He will be there to help you through it all. There may be times when you cannot make it to a church, however, if you can get on the phone with a friend and pray together, God is right there with you already working it out. Like it says in the Scripture below, God is in the midst of all your problems if you come together in His name and believe that He is able and will be with you.

Matthew 18:20 says, "For where two or three come together in my name, there am I with them." God wants us to worship together as much as possible because worshipping in the spirit is greater in numbers. Though circumstances may come where you may not be able to worship together, therefore, find a peaceful place in your home, call a friend on the phone, or have that person over to worship with you. Just praise His holy name and He will be right there. God will never leave you alone. So, stay positive and remember, *Change Your Mind & You Change Your Life!*

What Would You Do For God?

Friday: May 14, 2010

John 3:16 says, *"For God so loved the world that **He gave His one and only Son**, that whoever believes in Him shall not perish but have eternal life."* God loved us so much that He gave His only begotten Son. What would you do for God?

Janet Jackson sings a song, "What have you done for me lately?" What have you done for God lately? Have you obeyed Exodus 20, the ten commandments? Have you turned from your wicked ways? Would you give up the world to gain eternal life? Would you pick up your cross and follow him? Would you humble yourself and praise Him daily? After all the blessings that God gives us daily: *Waking us up each day, keeping a roof over our heads, providing in ways we thought was impossible and the most important one is giving us grace* and mercy, while showing His love by being compassionate and understanding. Forgiving us our sins each day and loving us with Agape' (unconditionally) love.

I say again, What would you do for God? Thinking about it should not be an option! Keep a positive attitude and remember, *Change Your Mind & You Change Your Life!*

Challenges

Thursday: May 13, 2010

As we go through life's challenges we must continue to hope and trust God: To seek Him and glorify Him no matter what. We must meditate and pray always. God will always be there for those who diligently seek Him and who are righteous.

Always keep a positive attitude toward life during your problems and God will carry you through. Challenges are to make us strong in the Lord. The more challenges and trials we face, the more we rely on prayer and God's word. Never give up and never doubt because God will bring you out of any situation you encounter. He hears you when you call upon His name. Just like it says in the verse below:

Lamentations 3:25 says, "The LORD is good to those whose hope is in Him, to the one who seeks Him." God is good all the time and all the time God is good. Continue to keep a positive outlook on life by giving God the Glory each time you are going through challenges. Know that something great is going to happen to you. Therefore, remember, *Change Your Mind & You Change Your Life!*

Right On Time

Wednesday: May 12, 2010

Sometimes we get so discouraged and wonder if God hears our prayers in a time of need. We often pray repeatedly for the same things as though God did not hear us the first few times. I am guilty of this at times. As if God did not hear me the first time. Not having the patience to wait for the Lord.

You have heard the saying; He may not come when you want Him to, but He is *right on time*. It is true indeed. God works on His time and not on ours. He knows what we need before we ask Him. Wait after we pray and be patient. When we have done everything humanly possible about our situation then we must stand on the promises of God.

Remember the story of Lazarus and his sisters Mary and Martha. You can read the story found in *John 11:1-46*. How Lazarus was sick, and Jesus knew but He had to address other business before he went to help His friend Lazarus. Then Lazarus died and was dead for four days when Jesus left Jerusalem to go to Bethany where Lazarus waits. When Jesus arrives, Martha was glad to see Him, yet Mary was not because of her brother's death. She felt like Jesus could have come before her brother died to heal him. Nonetheless, Jesus was hurt and wept because they did not believe in the Glory of the Lord. The Scripture in John 11:25-26 states, "Jesus said to her, I am the resurrection and the life. He who believes in me will live, even though he dies; and whoever lives and believes in me will never die." Do you believe this in your heart to be true?

Sometimes we act like Mary. When problems are not solved right away we get an attitude and keep to ourselves. Or we become angry when we know someone who can help your situation, though they will not do it right away. We want it done when we want it done, having no patience. We must always believe in the Word of God and his promises. And no matter how much trouble comes our way know that God is there to help us. *He may not come when we want Him to but He's always Right on Time!* So always keep a positive attitude and remember, *Change Your Mind & You Change Your Life!*

Footprints

Tuesday: May 11, 2010

This is one of my most favorite and beautiful poems:

Footprints

One night a man had a dream. He dreamed he was walking along the beach with the LORD. Across the sky flashed scenes from his life. For each scene, he noticed two sets of footprints in the sand: one belonged to him, and the other to the LORD.

When the last scene of his life flashed before him, he looked back at the footprints in the sand. He noticed that many times along the path of his life there was only one set of footprints. He also noticed that it happened at the very lowest and saddest times in his life.

This really bothered him, and he questioned the LORD about it. LORD, you said that once I decided to follow you, you'd walk with me all the way. But I have noticed that during the most troublesome times in my life, there is only one set of footprints. I don't understand why when I needed you most you would leave me.

The LORD replied, "My precious, precious child. I love you and would never leave you. During your times of trial and suffering, when you see only one set of footprints, it was then that I carried you."

Never doubt the Lord. When the road seems hard to bear just know that God is there to help you. He will never leave you or forsake you. He will carry you through. Keep a positive attitude and remember, *Change Your Mind & You Change Your Life!*

Angry Sleep

Monday: May 10, 2010

How often do you get angry with someone or get into a bad argument and say I am not talking to them for a long time? Maybe discontinued a phone call because of something a person said that rubbed you the wrong way. Then before you could resolve your differences that person was no longer present. Moreover, you feel bad you were never given the opportunity to apologize. Deep in your heart, you feel the person knew you loved them or cared, yet the last words you said to them might have been harsh. And it just wears on your mind forever.

Well, my grandma used to tell me, never let the sun go down

being angry at someone because you don't know when the next time you will see them. Forgive them, she said. I call that *angry sleep.* Going to sleep angrily while being upset with someone. It could be a friend or family member. It does not matter who it is, if you have not come to an understanding before you retire for the night. Yeah right, I used to say. It was always a problem for me when I was young to forgive or apologize to someone. My grandma used to spank me just to make me apologize to someone. Before I get a spanking I would tell her forcing me is not a sincere apology. In my heart, it was not my fault anyway. However, my grandmother still made me say it.

Ephesians 4:26-27 says, "In your anger do not sin. Do not let the sun go down while you are still angry, and do not give the devil a foothold." Other verses to read are Psalm 4:4, Psalm 37:8, and Mathew 5:22. You do not want the devil to get the glory. The next time you feel upset with someone, end the conversation with, *I still love you no matter what we disagree about, and I will talk to you soon; have a blessed day.* Not only will you be blessed, despite it all, but the person on the other end will also be blessed. So, stay positive, prayerful, and remember, *Change Your Mind & You Change Your Life!*

Do You Love Your Mother?

Sunday: May 9, 2010

Happy Mother's Day

Every Mother's Day I think of the song *"I'll Always Love My Mama."*

65

The part where it says, *you only get one girl*, made me realize you only get one mother so enjoy her while you can. "Children, obey your parents in the Lord, for this is right. Honor your father and mother, which is the first commandment with a promise, that it may go well with you and that you may enjoy long life on the earth. This is a **promise** that God makes to children that you may enjoy a long life if you are obedient (Eph. 6:1-3)."

Here are Scriptures that speak about honoring your parents. Exodus 20:12 - "Honor your father and your mother, so that you may live long in the land the LORD your God is giving you." It is a gift God gives you to Honor your parents. Having a long life is an incentive for being respectful, obedient, mindful, caring, helpful, loving, and cheerful to your parents. Matthew 15:4 states, "For God said, *Honor* your father and mother and anyone who curses his father or mother must be put to death." Mark 7:10 says, "For Moses said, *Honor* your father and your mother, and *Anyone* who curses his father or mother must be put to death. Lastly, Exodus 21:17 mentions, "Anyone who curses his father or mother must be put to death."

Here God commands that you be put to death for cursing your parents. Death is a serious matter. So, watch what you say to your mother as well as your father. Always show her respect. There are more verses you can read: Mathew 15:11, 16-20, which talks about the child who feels they do not owe their mother any respect if they help in any way. It also states how people who look down on others who do not wash their hands before they eat are unclean. But the

Word reminds us that if you eat with unclean hands your food goes into the mouth into your stomach and out of your body. However, the things that come from the heart out of the mouth are what make a person unclean. For out of the heart comes evil thoughts like murder, adultery, fornication, theft, false witness, and blasphemy.

I used that Scripture for you to understand how we worry about the wrong things. Having clean hands is nothing compared to a filthy tongue. To love your mother truly is to be obedient to her and the will of God. Mothers are not perfect. They have plenty on their plates. Single mothers have even greater responsibilities such as working, paying bills, buying food, clothes, the car note, etc. Moreover, when their child has issues at school, they take off work and then try to stay stress-free. Being obedient to the scriptures are a small price to pay.

Do you love your mother? Have you ever surprised your mom by lending her a helping hand? It does not matter how old you get; you only have one mother in this life. Depending on your schedule, do you love your mom enough to massage her feet when she comes home from work or take her to get a pedicure; run her bath for her with bubbles or take her to the spa; have a nice meal waiting for her so she can relax from a hectic day or take her out to dinner?

Have you asked her how her day was and how she was feeling? Do you love your mother enough to be obedient to her and listen when she tells you right from wrong? When you were younger and she told you to respect your teachers at school, do not curse or swear, not to fight in the streets or at school, do not bully another child, and obey the law of the land by not stealing, killing, or joining a gang.

Parents can die of a broken heart due to excessive stress and pain in the heart. Make your parents proud of you by going the extra mile. Sometimes parents have bad days. However, do not let it keep you down. Stay positive and tell your mother how much you love her daily. You only get one. Remember, Change Your Mind & You Change Your Life!

Are You Listening?

Saturday: May 8, 2010

When I was growing up my grandmother would always have to remind me and my other siblings about important things repeatedly. One day she was discussing something she had already told us. I said to my grandmother, "Why do you keep repeating yourself?" She said, not everyone may understand what I am saying. Just because you are a quick learner does not mean the rest of your siblings comprehend. So, I must keep reminding them every day.

The Holy Spirit reminds us of the things we need to know. However, we keep going through life being angry, disappointed, or depressed. One reason is because we do not listen to His voice. Therefore, we keep making the same mistakes repeatedly.

Proverbs 1:33

"But whoever **listens** to me will live in safety and be at ease, without fear of harm."

John 8:43

"Why is my language not clear to you? Because you are unable to hear what I say. To listen, hear and understand what God is telling us we must pray and continue to read the Word. Those who have ears let them hear."

John 17:7-8

"Now they know that everything you have given me comes from you. 8 For I gave them the words you gave me and they accepted them. They knew with certainty that I came from you, and they believed that you sent me."

To understand God, you must want to do his will. Not just to glorify yourself but to glorify God by living righteous. Are you listening to what God is trying to tell you? Sometimes we need to go into our quiet place to meditate and pray. Asking God what it is He wants us to do and just listen. Wait on the Lord and He will direct your path. So, keep a positive attitude and continue to put God first in your life. And remember, *Change Your Mind & You Change Your Life!*

Who Said What?

Friday: May 7, 2010

Gossip can hurt one's feelings, start a fight or argument, be harmful to a person's reputation, and most of all, most gossip is not facts but lies. When I was small my grandmother used to say, if you do not have anything good to say about anyone say nothing, just be silent.

Never in the history of the Bible did Jesus ever gossip or talk negatively about anyone. Moreover, Jesus never spoke falsely about what God's word wanted us to do. For He is a God that is not deceitful. So, we should not speak falsely about others.

1 Corinthians 14:33 says, "For God is not the author of confusion but of peace, as in all the churches of the saints." God is love and peace. So, treat people the way you want to be treated. The next time you hear gossip, or someone wants to tell you what they said. Tell them what God told you. And remember, *Change Your Mind & You Change Your Life!*

Trouble Don't Last Always

Thursday: May 6, 2010

Sometimes we wonder why life seems so cruel and hard when we feel that we are doing the right things. We meditate and pray daily, treat people well, go out of our way for others, pay our tithes cheerfully, give God the glory and praise He deserves, keep our faith, and here comes trouble. Life can be going great, and trouble comes out of nowhere and slaps you right in the face. You fall and get back up and here comes another punch then another. Before long, you begin to question yourself. Before you know it, you begin to ask the Lord, did I do something wrong and forgot to ask forgiveness? Then you realize it is the trials and tribulations you are going through. Testing your righteousness like Job. No one is above being tested by God.

God just wants to know if you still remember Him. If you remember how good His grace and mercy have been. How much He's done for you without you asking. God just wants to know that you still love Him with all your heart, mind, soul, and strength, as much as He loves you. God said He is a jealous God. There are moments we get wrapped up in our own lives and may ignore Him, especially when life is going great for us. Like it says in the verse below:

Psalm 30:5

For His anger is but for a moment, His favor is for life; Weeping may endure for a night, but joy comes in the morning.

Though trouble comes it will not last always, if you just keep the faith. Tests are ways in which God promotes us. He wants to know if you can persevere through the storm. Will you grab your umbrella or stay in the house? *There is always a plan and purpose for your pain.* Just glorify the Lord and sing praises to Him. Do not be silent but give Him thanks. Just know that your *trouble* will turn into *tranquility* by letting Christ know that He is King of Kings and Lord of Lords. So, remember, *Change Your Mind & You Change Your Life!*

ORDER In The House!

Wednesday: May 5, 2010

If you've ever been to a courtroom or seen court action on television, when the case starts to get out of hand, attorneys are arguing or the room is out of order, the Judge hits the gravel and yells order in the court. Well, the same applies to your house. When the kids are doing what they want, you and your spouse may be having problems, dishes and clothes are starting to pile up. It is a sign your house is getting out of order. You notice you are losing control. This can lead to many distractions and headaches. 1 Corinthians 14:40 say, "Let all things be done decently and in order."

Just like we must have order in society with laws and our government to keep the peace. We must have order in our homes to have peace. Continue to meditate, pray, and have a positive attitude. And the next time your home gets out of control, grab your Bible and shout ORDER IN THE HOUSE! *And remember, Change Your Mind & You Change Your Life!*

Are You Too Busy For God?

Tuesday: May 4, 2010

How often do you just wake up and say, "THANK YOU LORD FOR EVERYTHING!" Just shout it at the world. Often, not often, never; or have you taken the time to think about all the things He has done? Or do you wake up requesting from the Lord, if you can help me with this or give me that or do I just need another favor from you?

Are we too busy for God to pray or take time out to say thank you? Start by spending one day a week praising Him for being so grateful? One day will turn into two days, then three, until finally you find yourself praising Him daily. Our God is an awesome God. He wakes us up every day. He provides shelter, food, and clothing. He makes sure you stay protected from evil while you travel to and from your destination. He provides you with financial stability. He makes sure you are healthy and provides medication if you are sick. He watches over you and keeps you through the night when you are sleeping by being a covering. He gives you the sun for light in the day so you can see your destination and the moon for nightlight. And most importantly, *He gave His Only Son that we might have eternal life!*

God is so busy doing for us; why are we too busy to praise Him for all the things He does to make sure we are happy? We can please God by giving Him praise for being King of Kings and Lord of Lords; Alpha and Omega, the beginning, and the end; The God of Abraham, Isacc, and Jacob; The Living God; Creator of Heaven and Earth. As I am writing this, All I wanna do is say, "THANK YOU LORD FOR ALL YOU'VE DONE FOR ME!" Take time and give God *all* the Praise. *And remember, Change Your Mind & You Change Your Life!*

Long Way From Home

Monday: May 3, 2010

When I was young I could not wait until I was old enough to leave home and start my own life. Once I turned 19 years old I was out on my own having a fun time. By the time I was 25, I had my first son. When I was 37, I had my second son, and my third and last child, who was my daughter at age 38.

During those years I had three children out of wedlock, thinking I was in love with their father. Moreover, I was too naïve and spiritually blind to understand what I was doing was not the will of God. But I thought I knew everything. Then at 41, I married a man who loved drugs more than me or most importantly, more than God.

73

Even after my divorce, I was still able to pick myself back up again and start fresh. Now eight years later, back at the same spot I started at age 49, *a long way from home.*

The Word of God does not come back void. Not living a righteous lifestyle comes with consequences. I used to tell my children there are choices you make, good or bad, that will determine your destiny. Despite all the things I have done, God is merciful and faithful. He never left me even when I felt alone.

If only I had listened to my parents (smiling). I feel like the Prodigal Son; Luke 15:11-32, *a long way from home,* feeling terrible about the mistakes I made. I realized that feeling down and depressed was not going to solve anything. As Donnie McClurkin says in his song, *We Fall Down But We Get Up!* That's what I am doing with my life. I am standing on the promises of God. He forgave me for all my sins. So, I am no longer *a long way from home.* Long as I got Jesus on my side I am not only right at home. I am where God wants me to be.

No matter how long it takes to go through your journey just remember Jesus will be waiting for you to come back home. Just try not to stay away too long because He misses you as much as you miss Him. And remember, *Change Your Mind & You Change Your Life!*

A Friend

Sunday: May 2, 2010

*Prov. 18:24. There is **a friend** that sticketh closer than a brother.*

What A Friend We Have In Jesus

Verse 1

What a Friend we have in Jesus, All our sins and griefs to bear! What a privilege to carry Ev'rything to God in prayer! O what peace we often forfeit, O what needless pain we bear. All because we do not carry Ev'rything to God in prayer!

Verse 2

Have we trials and temptations? Is there trouble anywhere? We should never be discouraged - Take it to the Lord in prayer. Can we find **a friend** so **faithful?** Who will all our sorrows share? Jesus knows our every weakness - Take it to the Lord in prayer.

Verse 3

Are we weak and heavy-laden, Cumbered with a load of care? Precious Savior, still our refuge - Take it to the Lord in prayer. Do thy friends despise, forsake thee? Take it to the Lord in prayer; In His arms, He'll take and shield thee - Thou wilt find a solace there.

~ Joseph Scriven, written 1855 ~

Joseph Scriven wrote this hymn because he had firsthand experience with heartache and devastation. As a young man, his hopes and dreams vanished on the day before his wedding when he watched in horror as the lifeless body of his beloved was pulled from the water where she had drowned. Sorrow overwhelmed him, yet in the months and years that followed, Joseph Scriven turned repeatedly to the only Friend who would never leave him, Jesus.

Though he battled loneliness and depression for the rest of his life, he never let go of the hand of his Savior. Joseph Scriven knew that Jesus cared and that He was acquainted with loneliness and sorrow. Still, he knew that he could take his grief to Jesus and find strength and peace that no one else could give. Years later he took what he had learned through his pain and put it into the words of a poem that we now sing as *"What A Friend We Have In Jesus."*

My friend, in your moments of trials, temptation, and hardship, turn to the *Friend*, Jesus, who is always there. Listen to His words as He speaks to you through the Scriptures. Be honest with God and with yourself about your thoughts and feelings. Spend time in prayer and experience the comfort of His presence. Seek His forgiveness when you stray from Him and His ways. Be encouraged as you remember that no matter what happens, He will never leave you. He will not abandon you. Let Him hug you close to His heart. Rest in Him and find peace for He truly is a friend that sticks closer than a brother! And remember, *Change Your Mind & You Change Your Life!*

Blind Faith

Saturday: May 1, 2010

Friday evening, I was approached by a blind man who needed my assistance. I was able to guide him in the right direction. We exchanged conversations while waiting for his transportation. Because of my kindness, he insisted on paying for my taxi. He pulled out a fist full of singles and gave me what he wanted me to have. Because of his *blind faith* and trust, he was not afraid that I would rob him. Hebrews 11:1 says, "Now *faith* is the substance of things hoped for, the evidence of things not seen." God wants us to be like the blind man. To trust Him without knowing the end results. Believing He will do what His Word said He will do. "So shall my word be that goeth forth out of my mouth: it shall not return unto me void, but it shall accomplish that which I please, and it shall prosper in the thing whereto I sent it (Isa. 55:11)."

In the Book, 2 Corinthians 5:7 says, "We live by *Faith*, not by Sight." God wants us to live by His Word and not by what we see first; To believe in His promise to us as Christians. To have blind faith, which is believing without seeing, is a blessing. So, stay in your word and always keep a positive outlook on life. And remember, *Change Your Mind & You Change Your Life!*

Monday, May 3, 2010

Death

Friday: April 30, 2010

At some point in our life, we are going to leave this world and go to a resting place. At least I know I am going to a resting place where there will be no more crying, sadness, depression, or hatred, just peace and love. You probably want to know what brought this on right? There has been so much killing lately, I want people to know that they must decide on whom they are going to follow, Christ or Satan.

We must live a righteous life on earth to receive our reward in heaven. Read Colossians 3 in its entirety and you will get a better understanding. Below are verses 1-10.

Colossians 3:1-10 Rules for Holy Living

"Since then, you have been raised with Christ, set your hearts on things above, where Christ is seated at the right hand of God. Set your mind on things above, not on earthly things. For you died, and your life is now hidden with Christ in God. When Christ, who is your life, appears, then you also will appear with Him in glory. Put to death, therefore, whatever belongs to your earthly nature: sexual immorality, impurity, lust, evil desires, and greed, which is idolatry. Because of these, the wrath of God is coming. You used to walk in these ways, in the life you once lived. But now you must rid yourselves of all such things as these: anger, rage, malice, slander, and filthy language from your lips. Do not lie to each other, since you have taken off your old self with its practices and have put on the new self, which is being renewed in knowledge in the image of its Creator."

Where are you going when you leave this earth? If you must think about it, then put to death the earthly nature and walk in the knowledge and the image of God the Creator. And remember, *Change Your Mind & You Change Your Life!*

About the Author

Hello, I am Dr. Vanessa Lynn Estes. I am a mother and a dedicated woman of God. I am a Pastor, Evangelist, Chaplain, author of *The Effectiveness of Praying and Fasting,* and founder of *God's Chosen Generation Church*, and *Women Within Ministries*, which helps women of Domestic Violence. I have three adult children and 12 grandchildren. Raising children, attending college, and having a ministry was a full-time job, which did not stop me from achieving God's plans for my life. That is why you must stay focused and "Press toward the mark for the prize of the high calling of God in Christ Jesus (Phil. 3:14)." We do not know all of God's plans, nevertheless, we aim to do His will by teaching and preaching to make more disciples of Christ.

My Calling

God called me to do His will in February 2009 during a challenging time in my life. I was going through depression. However, God became my strength in the storms of life. This is when I experienced the *Power* of God. It is in our weakness that God makes us strong. "And he said unto me, My grace is sufficient for thee: for my strength is made perfect in weakness (2 Cor. 12:9a)." God will give you His strength when you are in your weakest moments. He wants to show you that you cannot do anything without Him. "Greater is He that is in you, than he that is in the world (1 Jn. 4:4)." I thank God that the devil had already been defeated. Most of all, for keeping me in my right mind. When I was a little girl, my grandmother would say, "Pray daily for God to guard your mind."

I had backslidden and fallen short of the glory of God, not feeling that my prayers were often heard. This caused the enemy to creep in and take over. Separation from God is not God separating from you. However, when you live outside of His will, you feel loneliness.

When I started experiencing anxiety, I remembered the scripture, "Thou wilt keep him in perfect peace, whose mind is stayed on thee: because he trusted in thee (Is. 26:3)." I may have gone back into the world; however, I knew how to dig deep into my soul – in the depth of my mind. And at the bottom of my heart was the Word of God. Like Psalm 119:11, "I have hidden His Word in my heart."

From the time I was born, I attended church; therefore, I knew Christ. During my brokenness, He heard my cry within my heart.

"And He who searches the hearts knows what the mind of the Spirit is, because the Spirit intercedes [before God] on behalf of God's people in accordance with God's will (Rom. 8:27, AMP)." God searched my heart, reached down, and pulled me out of the pit of mental hell. "If I ascend up into heaven, thou art there: if I make my bed in hell, behold, thou art there (Ps. 139:8)."

Wherever you go, God will be there for you if you call on His name. Moreover, if you have a personal relationship with Him, He knows your heart and hears your cry without saying a word. God knew that I needed help fast, quickly, and in a hurry. I thank the Holy Spirit for never leaving me, even when I left the presence of God. I praise Him daily for waking me up every day and for showing me His grace and mercy, but primarily because of His compassion for His lost sheep. I always belonged to God, even when I became rebellious and decided to do things my way. I learned that there are two ways of doing things: the easy way and the hard way. Nevertheless, I needed to get back on course, *Reset* my life.

I wrote this blog in the summer of 2010 to keep my mind focused and on tasks. I hope others going through similar struggles can identify with me. Moreover, I can help someone by encouraging them to never let go of God's hand. Writing this blog kept my mind peaceful, and I wanted to share it with you to help you understand the importance of positive thinking. So, enjoy and keep your mind stayed on Jesus. "Thou wilt keep him in perfect peace, whose mind is stayed on thee: because he trusteth in thee (Is. 26:3)." I hope and pray that reading this book will help you to develop a way of thinking that will keep you in a positive mindset. And remember, *Change Your Mind & You Change Your Life!*

Scriptures for Peace

While on the internet, MSN, I found this story written by Martha A. Lavallie titled. "*10 Bible Verses That Will Comfort You When Life Feels Hard.*" As I read the article, I thought it would be something to help ease the mind and comfort our spirit. Therefore, I would like to share them with you.

1. 1 John 3:16 (NIV)

"For God so loved the world that he gave his one and only Son, that whoever believes in him shall not perish but have eternal life."

It tells you about God's incredible love for everyone. It says that God sent His only Son, Jesus, to save people. If you believe in Him, you can have eternal life, which means living forever with God.

It's a powerful reminder of hope and love.

2. Philippians 4:13 (NIV)

"I can do all this through him who gives me strength."

You're reminded that no matter how tough things get, you have the strength to get through them. It's about believing that with Jesus by your side, you can face any challenge.

It encourages you to keep going and trust in His power.

3. Jeremiah 29:11 (NIV)

"For I know the plans I have for you," declares the Lord, "plans to prosper you and not to harm you, plans to give you hope and a future."

Here, God is telling you that He has good plans for your life. It means He wants you to succeed and be happy. Even when things seem hard, you can trust that there's a bright future ahead.

It's a comforting thought that you're not alone in your journey.

4. Romans 8:28 (NIV)

"And we know that in all things God works for the good of those who love him, who have been called according to his purpose."

It reassures you that God is always working behind the scenes for your good. Even if something bad happens, God can turn it into something good.

It encourages you to trust in His plan and believe that everything will work out for those who love Him.

5. Matthew 11:28 (NIV)

"Come to me, all you who are weary and burdened, and I will give you rest."

In this invitation, Jesus is asking you to come to Him when you feel tired or overwhelmed. He promises to give you rest, both physically and emotionally. It's a reminder that you don't have to carry your worries alone; you can find peace in Him.

6. Psalm 23:1 (NIV)

"The Lord is my shepherd, I lack nothing."

In this verse, you are reminded that God takes care of you like a shepherd cares for their sheep. It means you don't have to worry about what you need because He will provide for you.

This verse brings comfort and peace, reminding you that you are safe in His care.

7. Isaiah 41:10 (NIV)

"So do not fear, for I am with you; do not be dismayed, for I am your God. I will strengthen you and help you; I will uphold you with my righteous right hand."

It's telling you to not be afraid because God is always with you. When you feel scared or uncertain, remember that He gives you strength and support.

This verse encourages you to boldly face challenges, knowing that God is right beside you.

8. 1 Corinthians 13:4-5 (NIV)

"Love is patient, love is kind. It does not envy, it does not boast, it is not proud. It does not dishonor others, it is not self-seeking, it is not easily angered, it keeps no record of wrongs."

You learn what true love looks like. It's about being patient and kind to others. Love doesn't keep track of mistakes or get angry easily.

This passage teaches you how to love others well, reminding you that love is about giving and caring.

9. Proverbs 3:5-6 (NIV)

"Trust in the Lord with all your heart and lean not on your own understanding; in all your ways submit to him, and he will make your paths straight."

These verses tell you to trust God completely, even when things are confusing. It means you shouldn't rely only on your own thoughts.

When you seek God's guidance and follow His ways, He will lead you in the right direction. It's about letting go and having faith in His plan.

10. Matthew 7:7 (NIV)

"Ask and it will be given to you; seek and you will find; knock and the door will be opened to you."

It's an invitation for you to ask God for help, seek Him in your life, and look for opportunities. It encourages you to be bold in your prayers and trust that God hears you.

When you reach out, you will find what you're looking for, whether it's answers, guidance, or comfort.

These words are more than just text; they are sources of hope and strength for many people. Each passage carries a message that can help you navigate life's challenges and celebrate its joys.

Spiritual Insight

If God is on our side, there is no one to fear. In Psalm 27, David talks about his enemies. Enemies do not have to be physical. The enemies that I had to deal with were the strongholds in my life: fear, anxiety, stress, discouragement, lack of joy or strength in my body, loss of appetite, feeling restless or tired, frustration, and lack of sleep. Some of you may have experienced these same symptoms. Others may have experienced suicidal thoughts, which I pray you seek help immediately. But let me say this to you right now, there is *nothing* too hard for the Lord (Jer. 32:17).

Psalm 23 is one of my favorite Scriptures. It reminds me of who God is in my life. He is my shepherd; He guides me by giving me directions. Here is a list of other Scriptures that will help you in your journey of renewing your mind: Psalm 27:1-14, Psalm 91, Romans 8:31, Ps. 95:1-7, John 14:6, and Micah 7:8.

Know that God will NEVER leave us or forsake us. When we feel lonely or think God has left us, He has not. The Master is always silent during the test; He is always quiet when working on our issues and managing our problems. Daniel fasted and prayed for 21 days before receiving an answer from God. The explanation is that the messenger angel, Gabriel, was on the way to deliver God's answer on the first day, but was busy fighting off the prince of Persia, who is an evil entity, a fallen angel. For that reason, know that delay is not bad, it is just not the right time.

Therefore, have patience, be still, stay humble, pray, read the Word, and let God stand in the gap for you. When you do these things, you will *Change Your Mind and You Change Your Life!*

www.ingramcontent.com/pod-product-compliance
Lightning Source LLC
Chambersburg PA
CBHW061707120626
46550CB00003B/1124

* 9 7 9 8 9 9 2 9 3 1 0 0 6 *